FROM BAD TO VERSE

Dianne Phillips-Zito

For my family.
You give me one hundred and one reasons
to smile and be thankful every day.

~♥~

This book won't make the A-List;
It hasn't Shakespeare's style,
But it's comfy and it's friendly,
And it may just make you smile.

So when things aren't going quite to plan,
Or your day gets worse and worse,
Just flip the pages of this book,
To go from bad to verse.

~♥~

We humans are a funny lot. Never be afraid to laugh at yourself.
There'll always be plenty of people happy to do it for you but
I've always found it to my advantage to get in first.

CONTENTS

THE APPRENTICE

I started in my new career all awkward, shy and meek,
I rocked up here on Monday so it's nearly been a week,
I'm already quietly confident that I know what I am doing,
For I can tell the difference with conditioning and shampooing.

The boss does all the colours and the perms and all the cuts,
I get to stand and watch her work until the salon shuts,
So I've gained a lot of knowledge in these five short days or less,
I've learnt the beauty methods that'll straighten out a mess.

I sweep the floors and tidy up, sort rollers from the prongs,
I'm not to pick up scissors or to touch the heated tongs,
But I get to write with pencil in the big book of appointments,
And sort the coloured tubes of dyes and leg wax from the
ointments.

Today was super quiet, no clients due 'til three,
There's a sale at the butcher shop and Madam said to me,
That she should've bought some rissoles while she had an hour
spare,
So perhaps she ought to dash around while no-one else was there.

"I shouldn't take too long, m'Dear, so can you mind the store?"
"I'll hold the fort," I proudly said, as she headed for the door,
She grabbed her bag and darted off, to purchase eggs and meat,
Before the butcher sold it all, along the other street.

But that was near an hour ago, the boss aint been back since,
I'm wondering just how long it *takes* to buy a bit of mince?
A lady rushed in frantically, she said she had a date,
She wanted all her hair curled up and said she couldn't wait.

I didn't want to let her down, or turn away new clients,
So I mixed the perm solution up; it's hardly rocket science,
I think it was two parts to five ... or was that figure higher?
I spread it on the woman's head and stuck her 'neath the dryer.

Then things got kind of heated; there was quite a bit of smoke,
Seeping out from underneath the towelling 'round her yoke,
I fobbed her off with coffee and a biscuit and a book,
But I had a dreadful feeling and was sort of scared to look.

The paramedics had a chat, when they stretchered her away,
They reckoned I should close the shop and take off for the day,
I think there could be trouble when my tardy boss returns,
'cause the odour wafting through the shop smells a lot like major
burns.

THE NEW ME

I've artificial fingernails
There's filler in my lips
Botox in my forehead
Liposuction from my hips
Staples in my stomach
A bottle bronzing tan
Hair extensions twisted in
Saline breast implants

My teeth have porcelain covers
False lashes, long and thick
My hair's dyed blonde and luscious
I haven't missed a trick
My ears have been pinned back a tad
My nose is slightly smaller
I'm standing on stiletto heels
So I look a whole lot taller

I've had a little nip and tuck
To remove some extra skin
I'm truly drop dead gorgeous
In this body I am in
With contact lenses on my eyes
I'm a poster girl for health
It's funny though, that lately
I just don't feel myself

SON OF A GUN

I'll tell you a tale that my ma told to me,
And after my story is done,
You'll say to yourself, that's quite a big yarn,
From an ordinary son-of-a-gun.

Out in the farmlands near Shepparton East,
Lived a hero, of sorts, to the locals,
Clever and witty and frightfully fit,
Just not much on looks or on vocals,

Gertrude McPhee was no ordin'ry lass,
She was born with a diff'rence or two,
She lisped when she spoke and she limped when she walked,
And had (most likely) an odd point of view.

But the locals adored her 'cause apart from the fact,
That she dribbled a lot when she drank,
For nigh on twelve years they had won the league cup,
And for that, they had Gertrude to thank.

Gert sure came in handy out there on the ground,
Every winter when football was tried,
Good old Gertrude McPhee was the one that they called,
'cause they all knew she wasn't one eyed.

Her eyesight *may* have been a questionable point,
And the one thing that always had got 'em,
For nobody knew which eye could see best,
The one on the top – or the bottom.

But her goal shots were brilliant and the team all agreed,
Without her they just wouldn't fare,
For no-one but Gertrude could scout out the field,
At ground level *and* up in the air.

9

She'd studied the game to a very fine point,
Gert knew every rule, good and proper,
And when out with the team, she had made it well known,
That no-one was going to stop her.

With a limp to the left and a lurch to the right,
Dived acrobatical Gertrude McPhee,
Covering all players and marking the kicks,
Running rings 'round the game's referee.

When the siren blared out at the end of the match,
It revealed they were victors once more,
And although they'd played hard and were trying their best,
It was Gertrude who'd settled the score.

So 'twas straight to the pub with the cup in their grasp,
To the marquee out back that they'd hired,
Celebrations were brought to a sudden full-stop,
When Gertie announced she'd retired!

A ripple of shock spread out through the throng,
Like a tidal wave hitting a pond,
And they all stood there gaping in stunned disbelief,
Just wondering why they'd been wronged.

But Gertrude just sighed and, they think, rolled an eye,
As the crowd became more and more wild,
Then she spat out aloud, at the top of her lungs,
"I'm giving up now BECAUTH I'M WITH CHILD."

Again, the crowd faltered and became deathly quiet,
'Til someone yelled, "Good *on* you; three cheers!"
So they drank for their win and they drank for their loss,
And they drowned all their thinking in beers.

Of course, rumours were rife on paternity matters,
But Gert's conscience was as clear as a crystal,
When she answered in cryptic to those who would ask,
That, "He woth quite a good shot with hith pithtol."

Yes, I do know the secret but I'd rather not say,
For when all is at last said and done,
Who am I to reveal what my mother would not?
I'm just an ordinary son-of-a-gun.

My sister's life is busy,
Filled with stress and work demands,
She tattooed clocks on both her palms,
For more time on her hands.

She always used to sleep in late,
Ignoring each clock's chime,
She built herself a bed of herbs,
So now she wakes on thyme.

THE OPERATION

The nurses handed me a gown, which was always on the cards,
That it would be too small by half – which it was – by several yards,
Stripped of all my corsetry and also of my pride,
My saggy bits drooped 'neath the hem, the rest flopped out the side.

No bigger than a pillow-case, exposing knobbly knees,
It left my backside cold and bare, subjected to the breeze,
They wheeled me on a gurney past entire populations,
Who'd seemingly lined the corridor to watch my tribulations.

They pumped me to the eyeballs with a liquid combination,
Of stuff that sent me gaga, just to add humiliation,
For even though, just half aware, of lights and blurry curtains,
I have a horrid feeling that I chatted up the surgeon,

I think they gave me something then, to make me *really* groggy,
The giggling nurses' faces went distorted, hazy, foggy,
And though I don't recall much more, about the operation,
That wondrous fog, that glorious fog, was beautiful salvation,

Or at least for just a little while, until my stupor cleared,
When I awoke it all came back, just as I'd kind of feared,
My eyes were fat and puffy and my chart was full of scribble,
And my hair was in a puddle on the pillow where I'd dribbled.

STRIKE A POSE

I'm going to be a model on a catwalk in Paree,
I've browsed a dozen glossy mags and feel it's meant to be,
They need someone pretty special and I'm pretty sure that's me.

When everyone is working hard from nine to five, surviving,
I'll be mingling at a gala somewhere, absolutely thriving,
Making packet loads of money pure and simply by arriving.

I wouldn't have to learn to drive; models don't drive cars,
They're chauffeured off to nightclubs and posh exclusive bars,
To mix it with the wannabees and up-and-coming stars.

They'd provide me with a stylist, and a makeup artist, too,
I'd always look amazing with their little tricks they do,
They can quickly add more cleavage using sticky tape and glue.

Yep, modelling's up my alley and I have myself to thank,
I find it super easy to make my mind a blank,
Shallow thoughts and vacant stares are money in the bank.

Walking down red carpets isn't difficult to do,
You pose, then stop to flick your hair and swivel on one shoe,
You clear your mind of everything like you haven't got a clue.

I'm only filling time in, at this part-time job, you see,
Practising to scowl and pout, which isn't hard for me,
I already know – it's simple – I've known since I was three.

I paid a massive fortune for an artisan to write,
A romantic Shakespeare sonnet on a single grain of rice,
I asked my husband what he thought,
He said it tasted nice.

LEONARD'S BIG NIGHT

Through eyeglasses perched on the ends of their noses,
Expectant eyes eagerly dart,
Awaiting the moment when Leonard comes out,
And announces he's ready to start.

Sometimes the quiet is broken by whisp'ring,
Then silence descends on the flock,
As keen ears aware of the smallest of sounds,
Overriding the tick of the clock.

Out back, the mood's solemn; they sip on their tea,
And nibble at cakes of their choice,
No-one dares cast a look toward Leonard's direction,
As he works on preparing his voice.

He sings up the scales, then he hums out aloud,
Adjusting his pull-on bow-tie,
And no-one would know he was nervous tonight,
If it weren't for the twitch in one eye.

With a glance at his watch and a flick of his hair,
Then a final loud throat-clearing cough,
Len turns on his heels and he heads for the door,
Now everyone knows he is off.

The audience tenses, applauding breaks out,
All agog are the ladies and gents,
"Raise your pens to your papers," booms Leonard to all,
"Weekly Bingo's about to commence!"

THE SUNNY HILLS RETIREMENT HOME ARGUMENT

Hattie May and Doreen Grace,
Met each other face to face,
Wheel to wheel and toe to toe,
Fluffy slippers poised to blow,
"Move your carcass," Hattie spat,
"So help me or I'll knock you flat,"
Doreen retorted, "Battle-axe,
I'll pump your ears so full of wax,
That you'll hear less than you do now,
You mouldy oldie, wrinkly cow,"
"Let me pass, Old Crusty Knees,"
"Not on your Nellie, Stinky Cheese,"

The two mad crones were so enraged,
For six whole minutes war was waged,
The reason for their grand debate?
Harold Selkirk – room One Eight,
Who appeared in slippers with a wobble,
To proudly view this public squabble,
"They're fightin' over me," he smirked,
As people in the hallway, lurked,
And on their canes invariably leaned,
Until a male nurse intervened,
"Back to your rooms, enough's enough,
Go finish crochet, cards, and stuff,"

And then added in more forceful tones,
"You're not to block the hallway zones,"

The residents started to disperse,
Still listening to the women curse,

Harold teetered toward his prey,
This little fight had made his day,
"I may be old but I'm still wanted,
And if you've got it, you should flaunt it,
Come ladies there no need to bicker,"
It was pure delight for his old ticker,
"And though it don't seem too profound,
There's heaps of me to go around,"
At this the women gaped, astounded,
It had them stumped, confused, confounded,
"What'd he say?" snapped Hattie May,
Doreen Grace looked Hattie's way,

She shouted back, "Well blow me, Jim,
He thinks we're wrangling over him!"
Their wheelchairs just about collided,
"You foolish codger," Doreen chided,
Poor Harold was taken so aback,
He nearly had a heart attack,
He'd overhead them late last night,
And knew they'd said his name, all right,
Hattie coughed, then turning red,
"We're arguing for your *room*," she said,
Then Doreen shouted, almost barked it,
"We want your room when you have carked it!"
But y'know, despite their best (or worst) intentions,
It eventually went to Myrtle Jenkins.

My cross-eyed boyfriend cheated,
A fact he'd not denied,
The entire time he'd dated me,
He'd seen *her* on the side.

*During their travels around Australia my parents brought back a
leaflet on the Chinchilla Melon Festival. This was my entry for its
poetry competition back in 1996 which earned 2nd place.*

MELANCHOLIA

"I've always loved me melons, lad,"
I told me first-born son,
"Me melons is me pride and joy,
Each and every one."

"I fondle and I sings to them,
I pat and polish, too,
I pampers and protects 'em;
I feeds 'em chooky poo."

"And I vow they loves me back, boy,
They grows so big and fat,
It's a shame to 'ave to sell 'em,
I 'ave to tell you that."

"But now it's harvest time again,
What blinkin' rotten luck,
I'll shed a tear or two, or more,
When I loads 'em on me truck."

"I met your ma through melons, son,
(though 'er father had a fit)
I said, 'I really likes your melons'
And she smiled and that were it."

"Two days later we was married,
nine months later you was born,
You owes your life to melons, boy,
Not rhubarb, rice or corn."

"Just good old fashioned melons,
The more the blinkin' jollier,
So spare a thought on market day,
for me and me melon-cholia."

DYSLEXIA IN THE DESERT

A long tyme bak, an age ago, when I was yuong and prettey,
I letf my littel village for avdenture in the city,
As a diplamot's asstisant, I got to travel widely,
It dident seem to faze my boss, that I have diksleksia – mildly.

It's a quirky litltle prblem, where some werds get mixd or bent,
And intsead of looknig regular, they go where they have went,
"Carmel," he'd often say to me, during casual natters,
"It's the prerson that you are inside, that onlly truley matters."

"Always try yorr very best, even *if* you try then fail,"
Dere Reeder, I am tellnig you, there's a morall to my taile,
One time in outer-somewair, where the sand could cooke a cayke,
I was aksed to prosess paprwerk for an old and lusty sheik.

His emales startid fine enuff – polite, should truth be tolled,
But it soon became apparrennt he was gettign way too bold,
"I want my sexy Caramel, in my tent out in the dunes,
Where I'll woo her and carress her by the glowing desserrt mune."

"I will kiss my sexy Carmle, where I kno she's not bean kissd,
And I'll cover her in syrip and ..." (Well, I'm sure you get the gist)
I did my best to give him whot he wonted for the nihgt,
He had sum verry strainge requests but I thikn I got them right.

I hope he liked the camel and that she didn't kik or spit,
When he tryed to lick the icecreem from beneeth her furry pits,
I trust she dident trampel him – thay say that true love hurts,
But I wontd that old lustey shieke to get his just desersts.

My Granddad's boating business,
Needs some help to stay afloat,
He's asked us all to hunt around,
To find the perfect boat.

He wants a showroom gimmick,
To attract the crowds to buy,
He decided it should be an ark,
I said I Noah guy.

MEMORIES

I often think of you and me, that time we got together,
You promised me a world of bliss, said love would last forever,
Remember?

The merging of our souls, you said, would bond us like cement,
But the merging of our bodies, was what you really meant,

That week was one in millions, (well, until the day you split)
I turned to see your morning smile but you'd done a moonlight flit.

I called you one week later, oh, no not to rant and curse,
Just to ask if you had seen the savings from my purse.

Pregnancy was soon confirmed, I felt like such a fool,
I sent you notes; the quins did well, throughout their years at school.
Remember?

All that, despite my lack of funds on an insubstantial pension,
Daily struggles for our bread, the constant stress and tension.

And when the children left my nest, I had to reinforce,
My confidence; I trained again, and did a nursing course.

All those draining hours I spent, bent over books of text,
To qualify to treat the sick, and then, what happened next?
Do you remember?

You staggered into hospital, in this ill and sorry state,
And now I'm the nurse in charge of you;
Do you believe in fate?

I do. And I remember; I remember *every*thing!

THE RIGHT WRITE

The crossword book lay open,
On the pillow by the clock,
While Sadie tried to figure out,
Three down, to fill the block.

"Say, what's a word for myriad?"
"It means a bloody heap,"
Groaned Edgar from beside her,
As he tried to get some sleep.

"Oh good, this fits!" said Sadie,
"Only one more to complete,
So what's this word, 'encounter,' mean?"
"It's another word for meet."

"Terrific!" squealed the woman,
And like a light was dawning,
She had a great idea to try,
At work come Monday morning.

She turned up bright and early,
She set about her target,
To attract a better clientele,
For her boss's 'upper' market.

She cleaned the butcher's window front,
The 'Minced Meat' sign came down,
And in its place she posted,
"Encounter – five quid per pound."

THE B&B DREAM

My enterprising husband went and sold our family home,
For a business we could run – just him and me,
But despite my protestations and a scarcity of funds,
He bought a dodgy, rundown B&B.

"We're going to live a lifestyle that we've never had before,"
Grinned Richard as they handed him the keys,
He hung his framed self-portrait in the front room of the house,
I scrubbed the grimy floors on hands and knees.

Richard said a seaside theme would calm our frazzled guests,
They'd appreciate a nautical delight,
He gathered seashells at the beach and tested different wine,
I stayed up painting walls throughout the night.

I'm out of bed and showered by the crack of every dawn,
There's a load to do and time does get away,
I don't sleep in like Richard does; he needs his full ten hours,
But one of us must organise the day.

The tables have to all be set before the guests stroll in,
For their morning coffee hit, or pot of tea,
I get the eggs and bacon done and cook assorted meals,
Yes, Richard gave the breakfast job to me.

He says he's more the thinking type, not one for manual tasks,
So I fill the vases full of fresh cut flowers,
I check the bookings, clean the rooms, I wash the towels and bedding,
Then sanitise the toilet bowls and showers.

Richard's very helpful, pointing out the jobs I've missed,
He's proud of being Captain of his ship,
To find an errant spiderweb or random speck of dust,
Would be a sign of letting standards slip.

He grandly welcomes visitors, smiling, shaking hands,
He chats to them of weather and of sport,
I fetch the luggage from their cars and haul it up the stairs,
While he sits behind the bar and doles out port.

Our visitors love Richard; he's a hearty friendly host,
Regaling all with stories, fun and witty,
He'd make an expert yachtsman – he's so full of puff and wind,
Which seems to me, a monumental pity.

When I'm sweating in the laundry or scouring out the oven,
I dream of all the things I plan to do,
With the money I've been stashing from the profit that is made,
Because *I'm* the one who does the banking, too.

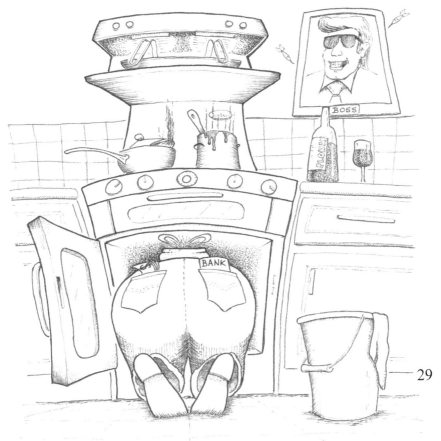

IN A BIND

Norm read the ad with interest, it piqued a little nerve,
This could be the very thing, to give him back his verve.

"Flagging stem or drooping? For a reason-able fee,
I can help you stiffen, phone triple five eight three."

A moment's hesitation, then a shot or two of gin,
Norm pressed the polished doorbell, and was warmly beckoned in.

The sexy red-haired beauty, said she'd go and change her dress,
"We'll go out in the garden, for we'll no doubt make a mess."

Exceedingly excited, he stripped down to the buff,
Whipped out his rubber cat mask, and the ropes and fluffy cuffs.

He bound himself (just loosely) to a shady clump of trees,
When to his shock, she reappeared, in gloves and dungarees.

"I thought you had some problems, with your roots ... er ...
of potted plants?"
Said the blushing garden expert, to the man without his pants.

Norm no longer answers ads, and won't come to the door,
He says he isn't looking for excitement any more.

He's become a bit reclusive, won't talk upon the phone,
His voicemail firmly states, "I'm tied up right now. Alone."

He wooed her for her beauty,
She chased him for his cash,
Love was never mentioned,
In their race-to-altar dash.

She married him for money,
He married her for lust,
But she was frigid, honey,
And his companies went bust.

WHEN I MOVE TO PARIS

One day when I'm old and no longer have ties,
I'll be down to the airport and gone,
I won't pack my bags, take a toothbrush or comb,
I'll just leave in the clothes I have on.

The day that I take all my dreams on a ride,
I will fly them to Paris at nine,
I shall sit on a balcony feeding the birds,
Flamboyantly spilling my wine.

The bakers will smile at this crazy old hag,
Scoffing frogs' legs with garnish and jam,
They will offer me crepes and those smooth custard tarts,
Saying, "Per'aps a croissant for Madame?"

I shall waltz through the Louvre with my spectacles off,
Squinting at artwork on view,
I'll point at the nudes and declare, "Ahh, Gauguin,"
"I knew it at once, didn't you?"

When bored with the Left Bank, and perhaps, of the right,
Or the crowds on the Champs Elysée,
I shall sit by the tower in a long sequined frock,
Pretending I'm famous. All day.

I will flounce along avenues shouting, "Bonjour,"
To the tourists who'll doff their berets,
I'll buy artwork and breadsticks and postcards and cheese,
And forget to keep track of the days.

I won't be that Gran with the house full of cats,
Nor the one hoarding teabags and plants,
I'll be morally bankrupt, eccentric and wild,
Enjoying my leisure in France.

A CUT GLASS ACCENT

I'd saved up all me pennies and I'd booked me two-way ticket,
I was anxious for the trip ahead – but yous'd never pick it,
I've watched a lot of Customs shows; they spot a nervous mood,
So I ticked the proper boxes and I didn't smuggle food.

I'd binned me bottled water and me boiled picnic eggs,
'Cause I didn't want the sniffer dogs come sniffin' round me legs,
The long haul flight was overnight and all the next whole day,
They brung us food at intervals on fancy plastic trays.

'Til there I was in England in a temp of 24,
I pulled me jumper 'round meself and headed out the door.
I'd just stepped outta Heathrow on me first grey London day,
But it musta bin me accent, that gave the game away,

I was spotted for a tourist before I'd cleared the gates,
The rip-off merchants pounced on me and upped the normal rates,
Me taxi drove in circles 'til his meter near exploded,
We finally pulled up near the Thames; me bags and me unloaded,

Charged double for me tiny room, and triple for me dinner,
I'd have to budget not to eat – at least I'd soon be thinner,
It could'na bin me rubber thongs or Aussie palm tree shirt,
The stickered suitcase, or me tan, or green and yellow skirt,

Nope, it musta bin me language, that set meself apart,
From all them other passengers right from the very start,
I tried to go unnoticed, lookin' like I was a local,
But I fear me voice has let me down; I curse me Aussie vocals.

So ai've hed to change the way ai talk to blend with other folk,
Or go bek to Orrstrarlee-ah completely stone coald broke,
Ai've storted talking posher, with a haccent like cut glorss,
So oivryone will think ai'm from the British upper clorsse.

They stare at moi so strangely now, (ai'm sure it's with respect)
I look elite with voice to match, just like whun would hexpect,
Ai'll bet they think I grew up rich and prive-ee-ately skewelled
They won't dare rip moi orff no more; this Aussie won't be
foowelled.

My set designer boyfriend,
Was on a downward lean,
They sacked him from the theatre show,
He didn't make a scene.

WHEN THE SHOW'S OVER

Strobe lights pulse and flicker, a disco ball rotates,
Eyelashes long and glittery, are what the night dictates,
Bold red lips in a face of stone, a face with no romance,
Just five more minutes up on stage, a grind, a lunge, a prance.

Money shoved in cleavage that isn't really there,
But all pushed high and out and up to make a stunning pair,
Gyrating on the dais, legs long and silky smooth,
Men get louder, more obscene, with every thrusting move.

Grubby threadbare carpet, spilt beer and rank cheap wine,
"Don't touch the dancers," printed on a dozen grimy signs,
The music stops, men shuffle out, a few odd drunks still cheering,
Stars retreat backstage to strip off memories and earrings.

Hair un-teased, the sparkle doused, the makeup wiped away,
Costumes hung, stilettos packed, the end of another day,
"Terrific show, old Harry, mate, far more than they deserve,"
"Yep, seeya back here tomorrow night; you drive home safely,
Merv."

THE SUNNY HILLS RETIREMENT HOME COMPETITION

Doreen was not the sort to lose; the same with Hattie May,
First to breakfast, first to bed, competing every day,
The two old biddies whizzed around, creating quite a laugh,
Among the other residents and weary Aged Care staff.

When Doreen knitted up a scarf, and then a fuzzy sweater,
Hattie May took up the wool, determined to be better,
She countered with a hat, some mitts, and followed with a run,
Of baby booties, socks and vests so as not to be outdone.

"I cannot stand this one hour more," announced the frazzled man,
In charge of patient welfare, "so I've come up with a plan,
To stop these ladies fighting and making me depressed,
We'll hold a competition with the winner crowned as best."

"I'm sick and tired of looking at their faces, gnarled and bitter,"
So Sunny Hills provided wool, one ball to each old knitter,
They gnashed their dentures, drooled and scowled, each sat beneath
a lamp,
Whilst witnesses stood round about, to see who'd be the champ.

Knit one, Pearl two, and double knot (or whatever it involves)
Dropped stitches, taking up the slack and poking back through
holes,
Twist over, in and under, and the tension that demands,
And the ribbing and the cabling and the blur of busy hands.

The clacking of the needles and the sweating of the brows,
Enthralled the dumbstruck audience – but not for several hours,
For in less than thirty minutes they had got their champ at last,
Hattie took the victory; Doreen had been outcast.

My cousin was hit on the head with some books,
After which he was never the same,
He shouldn't have practised D.I.Y.
He had his shelf to blame.

THE WAITING ROOM

I chatted with old Gladys at the clinic near the mall,
She confided as we waited for the nurse to give a call,
Her piles were problematic, and her veins were getting thicker,
That I could thank my lucky stars I didn't have her ticker.

"While *you* sit there in comfort, Dear, my pain is off the chart,
May you never know the turmoil of a palpitating heart,
Yet here I suffer patiently while others less afflicted,
Can carry on regardless, their lifestyles unrestricted."

"Spasms daily torment me from earlobes through to hips,
Which isn't something that you'd hear, from *my* judicious lips,
I bear these burdens silently, there's nothing good to gain,
From sharing woes or agonies related to my pain."

"I despair of hypochondriacs, continually groaning,
My back gave out six years ago, but *do* you hear me moaning?
I'm sure some make their ailments up; a trait that often rankles,
They'd not be quite so vocal if they suffered my weak ankles."

"I'm not the type to gripe or whine, about my daily plight,
I rely on medication to help me through the night,
I've been especially lucky to get rare prescription pills,
Called "Placebo" medication that assists my unique ills."

I'm puzzled as to how you say you just walked in off the street,
When doctor's always busy – an appointment's quite the treat,
Anyway, I'm low on hematoma now, or it's possibly my plasma,
I only pray he sees me first so I don't catch your asthma."

41

This poem was inspired by a One-word challenge on the 'Talkback' website through UK Writers' News several years ago. In this instance, the word was 'eclipse' and this was my eventual take on an idea totally unrelated to planetary alignments.

ECLIPSE

Auditions for the pantomime were held at Daisy Brown's,
The queue snaked out across her lawn as folk from nearby towns,
Turned up to show their talents off, to try out for the parts,
In the annual stage production, by St. Luke's Performing Arts.

Gordon juggled billiard balls but sadly, dropped all three,
And Moira drank a glass of wine, a puppet on her knee,
Mr. Campanetti sang a powerful cantata,
Accompanied by his nervous partner's violin sonata.

As hours drew on, the names were ticked off Daisy's running sheet,
Until the last auditionees walked in from off the street,
"I've only got two places left," said Daisy, then, "Of course,
You two can have the front and back of St. Luke's old panto horse."

Thelma stood by Walter and she squeezed him on the shoulder,
"We used to get the starring roles but now we're getting older,
It may be time for Walter 'ere, and me to step aside,
But we'll do our best to play the 'orse with dignity and pride."

The opening performance, was the highlight of the year,
And when the horse came trotting out, the crowd let out a cheer,
Old Walt and Thelma never missed, a step or curtain cue,
Which is why the critics praised them with a wonderful review.

"We've never seen a panto horse with such coordination,
Walt and Thelma really earned our fondest adulation,
And when we asked this thespian pair, to share their acting tips,
Thelma said, 'I do the clops, and Walter ... well ... 'e clips.'"

THE URBAN COWBOY'S LAMENT

It's a long way to the outback, from southern New South Wales,
Where he'd sat behind a desk most of his life,
He had a mid-life hankering to live his cowboy dream,
That did not include his unsuspecting wife.

He up and quit his stable job and bought a clapped-out Ford,
With the money he'd been stashing in a jar,
While his wife was sleeping soundly, he crept quietly to the shed,
And shoved a few belongings in the car.

He had penned a farewell letter which he'd stuck upon the fridge,
With a magnet that had once held children's art,

"You may well think this is sudden but I'm leaving for the bush
For I've always been a cowboy in my heart.

"You've been a kind, supportive wife for all our married life,
I've never heard you once complain or moan,
But cowboys can't be tied and roped like ordinary men,
We need to spread our wings and fly alone."

With artful flair he scored his name across his exit note,
Took a final goodbye look around the room,
Plugged a dodgy tracker in the dashboard of the car,
And set the destination point for Broome.

An avid fascination for the sunsets and the views,
That had for many years been on his mind,
Was soon replaced by gasping thirst, red dust, and searing heat,
And a cloud of black exhaust fumes right behind.

Roos pricked up their startled ears at loud and screechy songs,
Whilst unfazed at roadside's edge the cattle lurked,
He shouted tunes from Johnny Cash to keep himself awake,
For the wireless in the car had never worked.

A trip so long and lonely that he almost turned back twice,
Saw him carry on through landscapes scorched and harsh,
At last he stopped in Derby where he pitched a two-man tent,
In the van park called, 'The Entrance,' by the marsh.

He signed up for the rodeo, the novice riders' group,
Dressed in gear appropriately western,
From head to toe he looked the part in chaps and chequered shirt,
To become the man he knew he had been destined.

Courage quickly left him, though, when he saw the ride he'd drawn,
Even though the beast looked slow and fat,
And of course, he didn't last two seconds on that bull,
He fell and broke both arms, and that was that.

Now, in books and movies this would be, the place we'd leave the story,
A not-so-happy ending for the knowing,
But he was still in Derby in his tent and casts and slings,
Because real life has a way of keeping going.

Long suffering and abandoned, back at home in New South Wales,
His deserted wife was absolutely fine,
Coffee outings with the girls, spin classes at the gym,
Until his pleading voice came on the line.

"I'm sure you've missed me madly, Dear, but you know we foolish men,
How often we are reckless and mistaken,
I never should have left you with the mortgage and the bills,
But I'm broken now, and stirred, as well as shaken.

"It was just a bit of time out, Love, consider it a glitch,
But now having had some downtime on my own,
I've decided I'm more useful as a husband and provider,
... if you would kindly pay my fare back home?"

She thought about it long and hard, relenting with a sigh,
A budget no-frills flight was thence acquired,
He gave away his moleskin pants, Akubra and the boots,
The two-second urban cowboy had retired.

Back at home weeks later, his broken arms since healed,
He never once more spoke of how he'd slipped,
But his wife has hung his plaster casts upon the kitchen wall,
A reminder that his cowboy wings *were* clipped.

HANDY DAN

The dog won't put a paw inside his reconstructed kennel,
Not one of us can blame the clever guy,
We are all a little anxious in a quiet, nervous way,
Since Dan has taken up with D.I.Y.

His first few starter projects kept him occupied and happy,
We quite enjoyed the handmade dinner trays,
But when Daniel started watching all those renovation shows,
His hobby went from fun to fervent craze.

"We need a thorough upgrade," he declared with drill in hand,
A determined scowl upon his brow and lips,
Like a cowboy in the westerns, prepared for combat mode,
A tool belt hanging low across his hips.

That wonky bit of kitchen wall that no-one ever noticed,
Was 'rescued' with the aid of touch-up plaster,
But extensions to the bathroom and the bedroom walk-in-robe,
Have turned our tranquil life into disaster.

Dan pulled out walls and windows and embraced electric tools,
With such gusto that it left the family reeling,
He hadn't checked the blueprints or the building's basic structure,
So the bedrooms had a sudden loss of ceiling.

He propped up walls with wooden poles, a nail in to hold them,
With a frightening sense of "fix-it" on his brow,
Tiles cracked, the door frames warped but sort of held okay,
Which forestalled a full-on cave in – at least for now.

Dan has said it's temporary, so enjoy the night-time stars,
That are twinkling in the sky above our bed,
He says it's like we're camping out yet comfortable at home,
But I rather liked a roof above my head.

Our bathroom is more airy than it's ever been before,
We can literally say we've really seen it all,
For as we sit and ponder all the mysteries of life,
We can wave at neighbours through our toilet wall.

It would get a little chilly if we had to take a bath,
But Dan destroyed the wiring and the pipes,
So we're saving on the water bills and managing to stay fresh,
Using supermarket disinfectant wipes.

We hang the family washing on a line strung up inside,
From picture hook to kitchen pantry door,
The breeze flows through and dries it, there's no need to go outside,
And the drips help clean the dusty vinyl floor.

The children's science project earned top marks for nature studies,
Their teacher was amazed and made a fuss,
"They must have spent so long outdoors; their knowledge is
superb!"
But the secret is the creatures came to us.

Up from holes in floorboards and in through gaping cracks,
The creepy crawlies added to our trouble,
We all get close and personal when sharing space and meals,
Surrounded by bespoke designer rubble.

The dog has let us know that he is anxious and afraid,
By cowering under bits of fallen wood,
Quite frankly I am thinking that it's safer out than in,
And to me, his kennel's looking rather good.

THE COUNTRY WEDDING

The bridesmaids, three, set quite the scene, in orange tartan gowns,
Clutching at their red and pink carnations,
With sashes, gloves, and epaulettes in fluffy purple trim,
They'd stunned the sweaty summer congregation.

Some guests had put their glasses on to get a better look,
While others thought it best to take theirs off,
The groomsmen stood uncomfortably in vests and too-thick suits,
And snickered at the young groom's nervous cough.

The bride had brought her own idea of impact to the day,
She wasn't known for subtlety or flair,
But it's a bride's prerogative to get just what she wants,
Making every single choice from shoes to hair.

The beehive hairdos took a bit, of balancing to stop,
From leaning too far forward or toppling back,
But they'd practised walking slowly with their heads held on a lean,
To stop the up-dos falling off their stack.

Ceiling fans squeaked noisily from rafters overhead,
Within the humid confines of the church,
And when the vicar turned them up to cool the heated guests,
The bridesmaids' hairdos gave a sideways lurch.

The bride, whose veiled face was masked beneath a ton of net,
Walked in when cousin Eunice loudly sang,
She floated down the aisle in a puffy whirl of tulle,
That wrapped her ample body in meringue.

The newlyweds held hands and posed for photos out the front,
Under vivid blue, expansive, cloudless skies,
While women passed on gossip in the shade beneath the trees,
The men stripped off their jackets and their ties.

Aunty Pat and Uncle Ed owned property with lawn,
Where they'd set up tents and faded beach umbrellas,
Several cooler boxes full of ice and cans of beer,
Proved a magnet for the thirsty wedding fellas.

The budget conscious wedding pair had bought a half a cow,
Thinking that a barbie would be cheap,
So they could spend the rest of it to honeymoon abroad,
'cause the cost of wedding catering is steep.

The guests donated salads and a multitude of sweets,
They'd cakes and creamy trifles laid on thick,
The booze flowed free and quickly on the sticky muggy day,
'til folk turned green and started being sick.

Some chucked up near the gum trees; some threw up by the pond,
Poor Bertie never made it to the loos,
Others clutched at stomachs or clenched their bottom cheeks,
As they dashed to reach their cars between the spews.

The gaudy bridesmaids' dresses and the tablecloths and lawn,
Was a sight not often smelt or seen, down under,
The colour combinations mixed with chunks of who-knows-what,
And the odour of the fresh wet sprays of chunder.

The local Doc was overrun with calls throughout the night,
The magnitude of patients filled his diaries,
Home visits and the hospital, the clinic overflowed,
So he called a locum in to aid enquiries.

The wedding guests were crook as cats, except for Tina Dobbs,
Who then became the answer to the saga,
They asked her what she hadn't had that all the rest had done,
She'd just indulged in salad and a lager.

And thus, it pointed to the beef that Uncle Ed had cooked,
The meat was sent for testing to a lab,
Seems Ed had had some trouble when the fire hadn't lit,
So he'd poured a tin of kero on the slab.

It sizzled on the barbeque, it tainted all the coals,
It soaked the kindling, all the hardwood logs,
It wafted through the smoke that worked its way into the meat,
And made the guests as sick as rabid dogs.

It would've made the headlines in the local town gazette,
But for the fact the staff had also been,
Invited to the wedding, so they all went down like flies,
At the country wedding stuffed by kerosene.

BOYFRIEND WANTED – APPLY WITHIN

I've not been endowed with a model's physique,
I'm more cuddly and rounded and wobbly,
As I often have stated, the gym's overrated,
Athletics, a worrying hobby,
I laugh at those joggers, so skinny and gaunt,
No flab on their thighs or their belly,
While I'm cosy inside, with the week's TV Guide,
There's so much to look at on telly.

An ex beau of mine was most commonly found,
Trekking up and down hills in the rain,
I preferred to stay down, at the level of ground,
Where my lungs didn't cause any pain,
But off he would trot in his wet weather boots,
While frankly I just never risked it,
I watched from afar, in the warmth of his car,
With a packet of safe choccie biscuits.

Weekends like those ones got awfully bleak,
So I dumped him for someone more stable,
A chap who was quiet, and rather polite,
Someone static but willing and able,
He told me I'd look good in rubber,
And he fitted me up for a mask,
I went a bit blank, when he mentioned a tank,
But for love's sake I thought I'd not ask.

It started out fine and we shared for a month,
A romance I'd thought to be thriving,
Until he appears, with some flippers and spears,
And tells me he's booked us for diving.
This bod wasn't made for a wetsuit;
It prefers to be loose, free and splendid,
He couldn't believe, I'd give snorkelling the heave,
And thus, that relationship ended

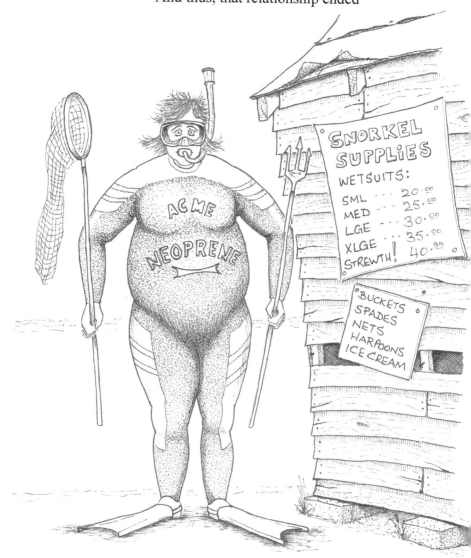

I dated a horsey type fella,
Well known for equestrian talents,
He took me out riding, but my saddle kept sliding,
And I never quite managed to balance,
The nag did its best to dismount me,
Which it did several times and quite fast,
Bruised from the falls, I ignored further calls;
That first date was also our last.

Which is why I have formed the opinion,
There's a particular type man that I like,
I've no time for canoes, or those reef walking shoes,
And you won't get me close to a bike.
I'm looking for someone who's normal,
A gardener, or collector of stamps,
Perhaps a designer, of velvet recliners,
Or tester of wheelchair-safe ramps,

He won't know his sails from his paddles,
Or pitons from racquets or skis,
If he likes to play chess, then the answer is yes,
I'm really not *that* hard to please.
I want someone who's happy to settle,
With a woman of non-sweaty sheen,
Who'll adore him forever, as long as he never,
Brings home a rowing machine.

About the Author ...

Dianne lives in Australia but has had many of her short stories (mostly in the dark/horror genre) published in both the UK and USA under the pen name, Anna Harris. This book marks the first publication of a poetry collection in her own name. She credits (or blames) her sense of humour to her much-adored family. When she doesn't have a laptop or a grandchild balanced on her knees, she is dreaming of escaping to a tropical palm covered island hideaway to contemplate her next story or series of poems. Dianne's email is: diannepzauthor@gmail.com

About the Illustrator ...

Kim usually works in pen and ink, mainly on commissions of caricatures of houses for special gifts. He also uses acrylics and loves to paint Trompe-l'oeil. His quirky line drawings appear as the successful 'Kim Moody' rubber art stamps available through Chocolate Baroque Ltd. Kim has edited the (now online) newsletter for the British Association of Decorative and Folk Arts (BADFA) for the past eleven years. He is happily married with three grown children and four super grandchildren. He retired from 'real' work in 2017 and now enjoys being an artist in his new home in Devon, England. Visit Kim's website at: kpmoody.wordpress.com and his Instagram at: kpm.illustration To discuss commissions, Kim would be pleased to hear from you via email at: kp9.moody@gmail.com

ACKNOWLEDGEMENTS

~♥~

I have my parents to thank for introducing me to the delight there is to be found in doggerel and ditties, rhythm and rhyme, and the nonsense and nincompoopery that has stayed with me my entire life.

While writing is generally considered to be a solitary pursuit, the publishing process takes a team effort. I would like to thank my family whose encouragement has allowed me the time and indulgence of getting this into print, particularly my stalwart husband whose patience and support has always been second to none.

I would like to acknowledge the many special friendships I've made over the years through the 'UK Writing News' group, *Writers Online*, (Talkback). Some of those madcap associates have become, and will remain, lifelong friends. They not only have a canny knack for dispensing expert tips and shouting support but can also be much relied upon to accommodate a 'virtual' hug whenever one is required. (There are far too many of you to mention individually but You know who you are.) More than a few of these poems took their first gasps of air in Talkback's, 'One Word Challenge,' and without them, this book would not exist, hence my sincere appreciation.

I would especially like to praise clever clogs, Kim Moody, whose witty illustrations have put not only a significant dollop of sparkly hundreds & thousands atop the cake but the icing as well as the cherry.

~♥~

Lightning Source UK Ltd.
Milton Keynes UK
UKHW020006030121
376246UK00007B/91